C000148618

Aaron Kent is a
and runs the M
winning press 1
awarded the Awe
for his poetry pamphlet ̶ ̶ ̶
has been praised by Gillian Clarke, J. H. Prynne,
Andrew McMillan, Andre Bagoo, Vahni (Anthony
Ezekiel) Capildeo, Abdul Kadeer El-Janabi, and
John McCullough. His recent books include the
full-length collection *Angels the Size of Houses*, and
a collaboration with surrealist artist John Welson,
Requiem for Bioluminescence.

Anthologies from Broken Sleep Books

The Plum Review

Edited by Aaron Kent

—

ISBN: 978-1-915079-63-3

—

brokensleepbooks.com

—

The authors have asserted their right to be
identified as the authors of this Work in accordance
with the Copyright, Designs and Patents Act 1988

—

Cover designed by Aaron Kent

—

Typeset by Aaron Kent

—

Edited by Aaron Kent

In support of

lay out your unrest

Broken Sleep Books
Rhydwen
Talgarreg
Ceredigion
SA44 4HB

Broken Sleep Books
Fair View
St Georges Road
Cornwall
PL26 7YH

Contents

The Plum Review

ed. Aaron Kent

Foreword

During National Poetry Writing month 2020 (NaPoWriMo 2020) The Poetry Society shared a writing prompt everyday, to which I replied with a parody of William Carlos Williams' *This is just to say*, a poem that had been successfully memed by that point. The prompts ranged from the Georges Perec-esque task to write poem where the only vowels allowed are the ones in your first name to fairly simple prompts such as 'write a poem using three things you can hear at midnight'. I wrote my favourite reply for the latter:

> I have heard
> the tapping
> that was rapping
> the chamber door
>
> and which
> was probably
> the wind
> and nothing more
>
> Forgive me
> it was a raven
> so he quoth
> 'and nevermore'

Rather than stop while things are good, always one to find more humour in relentlessly running a joke into the ground, I continued to reply to their social media posts with these parodies as time went on, utilising the safe familiarity of the 'plum meme'.

The idea to create an anthology of plum poems, though, then came from my desire to take the joke further still, to see if I could recruit some of my favourite contemporary poets to write their own version. Several of the poets included had done so in the past, particularly Rob Taylor who has had great success with some absolute GOAT plum memes, and others were approaching it for the first time.

In a time, though, where the cost of living crisis has left many iceboxes empty, with families struggling to find the plums to feed themselves and their children, I wanted to ensure this anthology gave back. It is important, then, that I thank the Trussells Trust, not just for partnering with Broken Sleep Books for this anthology, but also for being on the frontline of foodbanks, maintaining these unfortunately vital stations of nutrition in these difficult times.

I'd also like to thank The Poetry Society, who I reached out to in the hopes they didn't think they were being made the target of a joke. They were, in fact, fans of the memes, and had enjoyed my replies to their prompts. They were gracious enough to allow me to utilise their house format in the cover design for this anthology, and were immensely supportive.

There is a veritable orchard of plum-based parodies, responses, and memes within these pages, and it has been a joy to put together, to engage with the humour, tact, and intelligence poetry can and does offer. Every poet I approached was delighted by the idea of the anthology, and keen to offer a poem, which I think speaks to the desire of contemporary writers to both engage with charitable efforts and activities, and to also acknowledge and present poetry that doesn't always take itself too seriously.

This is just to say I have edited the anthology which you are reading, and which you were probably hoping started by page nine. Forgive me, the intro is three pages, so rambling and so meta.

— Aaron Kent

this is just to reply

correct. i *was* saving the plums in the ice box, you prick
if you'd even a hint of this fact, which you obviously did,
why eat them? not even just one, no, the whole fucking lot;

sweet and delicious they were, thank you for explaining
their flavours to me, me, who pinches their skins, sniffs
meticulously at market each week, to specifically check

for those qualities of sweet and delicious before carrying
them back in the basket, delicately placing them into the
ice box thus easing tomorrow's morning routine: wake;

wake up our children; make them their breakfast; get the
plums from the ice box; put fruit snacks in school bags;
school bags by front door; shoes on; coats zipped; a kiss

on each cheek - which you'd know, if you stopped staying
up late writing apology poems about eating the children's
fruit snack, again, which you mistakenly think i find sweet.

No one needs to say

Helloo Clarice
as they
slowly open
the refrigerator

Each panel
left empty
like some
Eisner-nominated pablum

Excuse me
while I throw myself
through the
fucking windscreen

This is just to say

I have bitten
the man
who was in
the fenlands

although
he had probably
tagged me
as human

Come pet us
we are ferocious
so wolf
and so furred

Just Ter She

Av et
Thi snap
That were in
Thi snap tin

That
Tha were probably
Savin
Fer snap time.

Soz.
It were reyt snap that.
Reyt snap.
Reyt snap.

Can I just say

(After Frankee's F.U.R.B)

I wasn't saving those fucking plums
I'd forgot about them
So bruised, icy, off-season

They only tasted sweet
Cause you thought I wanted them
Cause to you they tasted like me

This is just to say

I have eaten
the mangoes
that were in
your poem

and which
you debated
as exotic
signifiers.

Forgive me,
they were luscious
so golden and
sweet-fleshed.

This is just to say

A book no one reads
    or unlimited sequels
  'this is just to say'
'I repeat my themes'

This is just to say

This is to say that my mother's milk was scarce
An endless shaking of a palm tree with no dates

But my mother wasn't a virgin
Nor was God a witness to pain

The Armenian doctor who was sent to the camp said:
I wonder whether it is a direct cause of the war

To feign the milk that wasn't
My mother would wet bread scraps under the tap

My sister would cry and we lying down next to her
Would cry along

Forgive me, my mother would say

Forgive me for a body with no breasts

This is just to say

I have re-watched
season three of Succession
that you had
on NowTV

and which we'd
laugh at with tumblers
of champagne
and pizza

Hey Dad
you're gonna be so disappointed
um so
so fucking

This is just to say

You have eaten
the free school meals
that were in
the icebox

and which you
were probably
diverting
from foodbanks

Forgive you?
No. There are children literally starving to death in
this country, families rolling dice to decide who gets to
eat today, teenagers who are leaving school at sixteen
having never known what it means to eat three meals
a day. Put the food back in the damn icebox.

Because I wanted

something to eat
anything sweet
and cold I went
to Budgens for

fruit though I
hadn't eaten
all day and it
was unlikely

to fill the gap.
However many
times one person
says I'm sorry

and forgives
another doesn't
matter. I ate
the fruit and left.

Plume

I haven't eaten
anything
from the
earth

which u
were probably
trying to save
anyway

sorry princess
the air is
so thin
& so cold

This is just to say

I have drunk
the wine
I said I was
done with

that I swore
after another
night of remembering
nothing but night

that I wouldn't
touch   forgive
me   I'm so weak
and lost and harried of mind

Hemm Yw Hepken Dhe Leverel

(Kernewek translation)

My re dhybris
an ploum
esa y'n
gist rewell

hag mayth
eses ta orth aga
gwitha
rag hansel

Gav dhymm
esens i dentethyel
mar hweg
ha mar yeyn

This Is Just To Gloat

I have revived
the language
that was in
Cornwall

and which
you were
hoping
to murder

Forgive me
it grows yet
so fair
and so alive

This is Just to Say

(Leave Those Kids Alone)

'I killed a wood pigeon yesterday. I used my homemade catapult. I was hiding in the haunted woods behind the school that kicked me out. Don't worry it was a quick death. Probably painless but it's cool. I put the body in my pocket. Then I took it home and cooked it and forced my son to eat the heart.' Hey! What's up Doc? What are we doing here? We're in a squat above the butcher shop. You zoned out listening to this animal talk. Snap out of it. Don't piss him off. He's got the best stuff in town. Everything else is stepped on shit. We are pretty broken right now but it won't last forever. I'm gonna be so clean someday I promise I'm gonna be so good for you and the so sad world even though it's ending. But not today I'm afraid delicious forgive us this penny of fire on a sick man's scales. The last magic eight-ball. Then it's curtains with a bluish hue. Do you swear? No more getting high for me, no more getting high for you. He's bagging it. You're paying. I'm Turner's 'Ship in a Storm'. Hold your chickens. Love is coming. I can feel it in my plums.

This is just

This Is Just To Say

The ice between
my teeth
is plum red
when bitten.

Steel nails
jack hammering a
felled
Autumn sun.

Crush then
your surreptitious heart.
Unsweetened, and
so very cold.

Plum

downright induced engagement deep aplomb
   ruff plumage reflect sound formed
   asdic upforth victorious, singing
   turn away target leap over integrate
   pittance device, exact measurement
   another luminous umbrage timid grot

Oh Blue Century

You showed up sporting plums and shameless vacancy,
engaging in ridiculous fights with yourself like the air.

Now everything is money spiders and babbling vats of bluster,
crates of government promises stacked on splintered pallets.

Your falling fruit is brash and loud, century.
You present new forms of surrender, online iceboxes

to make me modern and lonely. Which is just to say
I've been eating your flesh too long, grow every day less sweet,

more cold. I talk with outside only by rearranging houseplants
in my window. Other means feel increasingly rude and futile,

like talking to a crowd of melting ice people.
How do I go back up? You are a plunging lift, century.

I hear the best thing to do in these situations is lie flat
so the force of impact will be spread across my pulpy body

but that makes it hard to peel myself from sofas,
to stop myself tuning in to see your weeks jangling past

in their clown cars, drivers waving zealously
to stop us watching all the giant blue flames.

This is just to say

I have taken
the migrants
who were in
the lorry trailer

the ones
you were probably
saving
for Rwanda

Fuck you
they are beautiful
so brave
and so kind

One day at a time

you have eaten
the all the ice cream
that were in
the freezer
that i was saving

and also the ones
you stashed
around the house
in unexpected places

and which
you were probably
thinking
would not be melted
before breakfast

forgive me
i preferred
life before your stint
in rehabilitation

there 'uv said it

'uv sooked the jooce oot
   the love spludge that
glistened in yer heartbox
   & which shiduve been
savoured fur forever
   & an eventide
lo siento / perdóname
   i didnae deserve yon gooey
gloriosity so returned masel'
   ti the begging end
of plumless glum
   salt knuckle fist in mooth
back ti the grid wafflin'
   teeth softenin'
delicious miserable
   work of lovin'
it grubby

Apocalypse Plums

I have franchised
the apocalypse
that was in
the hamper

and which
you were probably
texturing
to broadcast

Forgive me
it was trifling
so Solomonic
and so now

This is just to say

Even plums
won't stay delicious
in the fridge
for ever

they will
probably
not be worth saving
for tomorrow

Forgive me
saying the obvious
Anyway
I ate them

***

What plums?
I didn't see any in the fridge

Sorry
I don't know about "knowledge of good and evil"

I want trousers

***

It was Eton
the chums
that are in
the cabinet

attended
and probably
fucking
Oxford too

Forgive them?
They are devious delinquents
so rich
and so cold

***

I have eaten
the Prods
that were in
the Irish box

and who thought
they were probably
saving
Belfast

Forgive me
they were demagogues
so twisty
and so vile

***

Even
the plumbers
that were in
the iPad

wish
you were probably
shaving
before breakfast

for them
They were delirious
and witless
as oatmeal

Inflation

Piss is musty pay.

Just never do a run-on from the title.

I love Eton, their buns, their pickaxe an itch.

I know, you are probably saving for Christmas.

Sieve this later, neat as a trinket's reproach.

This Is Just to Say

for a former boss

I have gathered
the women
you tried
to destroy

and which
you probably
assumed
all but dead

Forgive yourself,
if you can
We are delicious
if not sweet, if not cold

This is just to say

I have eaten
the tories
that were in
first class

and which
you were probably
hoping
would fast

Believe me
they were unseasoned
so bland
and so cold

This is so's ye ken

(a Glaswegian slang translation)

Ah've scranned
they plooms
thit wur in
the iceboax

'n' thit
ye wur prob'ly
keepin'
fur yer porridge the morra

Forgee me
they wur braw
pure juicy
'n' pure baltic

This is just to say

I have plumbed
the depths
of your
being

which you
were probably
saving
for therapy

Forgive me
they were irresistible
so murky
and obscured

Dear Student

I shall be
another five

perhaps ten
minutes
I'm so

sorry to
be late
again
but this pain

au chocolat
simply could not
wait

Lump Anagrammics

Jay sits stoutish   though there is no place to sit.

> *I have eaten all the furniture*, the prime minister said
> to my dead brother.

> So minacious. So bold. So Eton. So plum.

This is just to say joys shit sits Uta.

> …And they were temporomandibular,
> …And they were psychoforay.

> Is Josi shut tasty?
> Josi ssh sui tatty.

His joy sit status turns the camera turns on you.

> Forgive me,

> you were probably saving.

> For breakfast,

I have smorgasboarded your war and published it in
a black deathbox.

And which so sweet. Hast its joys situ?
　　　Probably. Just Oasis shitty.

Beyond pisseries of cow parsley, beaten lumps,
　　　<Hiya! It joust SSTS.
　　　Justitia shy toss.>
　　　the doctor bears his refridgerating hand.

This is just to say…

　　　but my father's dementia
　　　unmemories the sentence.

Forgive me. It's like
　　　something eats away at me

　　　but I can't

　　　see it.

　　　And I can't
　　　kill it

　　　until
　　　it kills me.

Who could say this if not you? What is not justly said.

Plum lumps.

So cruel, so malicious.

[…]

What's the sentence?   I can't remember the sentence.

What's the word?   I've forgotten the word.

[…]

Are you trying to say goodbye?

Yes, that's exactly what I was trying to say.

This is just to say

I have taken
the crayon
that was in
the crayobox
and which
you would have
used
for a dinopoem

oh wait
this is one
dino
dinoooo

Fisk is Just to Say

A 'Fisk' coffin is an air-tight metal sarcophagus patented by Almond Dunbar Fisk in 1848. It was popular as a means of burial during the mid-to-late 1800s. Designed to prevent the spread of dangerous diseases, it kept bodies in an almost perfect state of preservation. A Fisk coffin usually incorporated a glass window, covered by a sliding hatch, through which the deceased's face could be viewed. The bodies of children have been found in such receptacles, so flawlessly unspoiled that they could almost fool the onlooker into believing they are merely sleeping. It is not known how most of these children died.

They pulled you
from the soil,
like a stone slipped out
of a sliced apricot.

You were stashed in
an iron skin,
bolted rivets
along your edging;

your stabbed seam
a bitten lip.
When they lifted
the shaming-hatch,

scrubbed the scum
from the glass,
your pinched face
peered back

through the smudge;
your cheeks two puffs
of pink smoke
suspended in

formaldehyde.
How did they hide
that dreaming smile
(hope-sick for just

one day outside
your child-shaped
ice-box), choke
in your fist-sized

throat the secret
your parents kept
of the hunger
that killed you?

Who do we forgive
for the caving-in
you cradled?
This threnody

we cannot say
is for that which
never grew,
still crushed

inside of you
like a sweet plum
whose taste
you never knew.

This is just to animate

1. Spider-Man

Ate the plums
They were yums
Your breakfast's gonna be lacking some
Oh so cold, oh so sweet
Your reserved icebox treat
Forgive me!
They were delicious!!!

2. Pinky and The Brain

I've eaten all your plums
Yes, eaten all your plums
The ones you were saving
For your morning yums
They tasted really nice
Sweet and cold and right
I've eaten
I've eaten all your
plums, plums, plums, plums,
plums, plums, plums, plums
plums
Forgive me!

3. Teenage Mutant Ninja Turtles

This is just to say I've eaten
The plums that were in the icebox
Saved for breakfast, please forgive me
They were so delicious
Sweet and cold!

This is just to say

I have eaten
the body of the world
and it was
so very sweet.

I have eaten
all of the fruit,
all of the trees,
and they were so sweet.

I have eaten
my body but I know
nothing of the
sound you call music.

When I wake up
the next morning
I will be made sweet.
I will have eaten.

This is not to be said

I have eaten of plums
satiated on tartness
iced of boxed benevolence,

you covet nature's gift

a hollow banquet

Now guilt
festoons my palate
chilled in nature's tears.

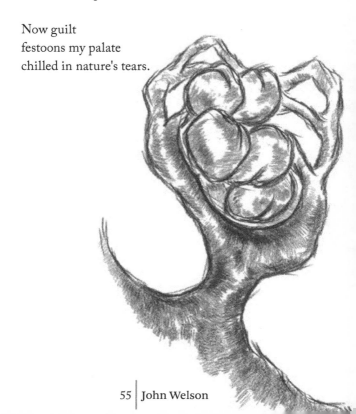

#ThisIsJustToSay

I retweeted
the plums-
that-were-in-
the-icebox

tweet
you had probably
already
seen

Forgive meme

an apology to aaron

this is just to say

i'm sorry I didn't
write a plum poem
for your anthology

cool & original, as you are
i just couldn't find anything
to say about plums

Dis Is Jus' T'Say

We are all
fucked
and overrated
I think I'm gonna be sick

from eating ice cream
or whatever we ordered
to stave off
the impending doom

I won't forgive
myself tomorrow
because
what would that achieve?

to say

this is
just to say
I really need
everyone
to stop riffing
on this
beautiful little poem
what has Bill
ever done to you
but write
his gorgeous poems?
enough!
into the icebox
with the lot of you!

Acknowledgements

'Plum' by J. H. Prynne first appeared in *Orchard* (Equipage, 2020)

'This is just to say' by Sam Riviere first appeared in *81 Austerities* (Faber, 2012) as *[45]*

'This is just to say' by U. G. Világos first appeared in *Ripe* (Danube Down Publications, 1967)

Contributors

Charlie Baylis is from Nottingham, England. He is the Editor of Anthropocene and the Chief Editorial Advisor to Broken Sleep Books. His poetry has been nominated twice for the Pushcart Prize and once for the Forward Prize. His most recent publication is *Santa Lucía* (Invisible Hand Press). He spends his spare time completely adrift of reality.

Jack Belloli is training for ordained Anglican ministry at Ripon College Cuddesdon. His pamphlet *Spandrel Routine* was published by Broken Sleep in 2019.

James Byrne is the author of the poetry collections *Of Breaking Glass* (Broken Sleep Books, 2022), *Everything that is Broken Up Dances* (Tupelo Press, 2015), *White Coins* (Arc, 2015), and *Blood/Sugar* (Arc, 2009). He is the international editor for Arc Publications.

Vahni (Anthony Ezekiel) Capildeo is a Trinidadian Scottish writer of poetry and non-fiction. Capildeo's eight books and eight pamphlets include *Like a Tree, Walking* (Carcanet, November 2021) and *The Dusty Angel* (Oystercatcher, 2021). They are Writer in Residence and Professor at the University of York, a Visiting Scholar at Pembroke College, Cambridge, and an Honorary Student of Christ Church, Oxford.

Jenna Clake's debut poetry collection, *Fortune Cookie*, received the Melita Hume Prize and an Eric Gregory Award from the Society of Authors, and was shortlisted for the Somerset Maugham Award. Her second poetry collection, *Museum of Ice Cream* was published by Bloodaxe in 2021. Her debut novel, *Disturbance*, is forthcoming from Trapeze and W.W. Norton in summer 2023.

A poem from **Rishi Dastidar**'s debut *Ticker-tape* was included in *The Forward Book of Poetry 2018*. A second collection, *Saffron Jack*, was published in 2020, and he is editor of *The Craft: A Guide to Making Poetry Happen in the 21st Century*; all three titles are published by Nine Arches Press. He is also co-editor of *Too Young, Too Loud, Too Different: Poems from Malika's Poetry Kitchen* (Corsair).

Carrie Etter has published four collections of poetry, most recently *The Weather in Normal* (UK: Seren; US: Station Hill, 2018), a Poetry Book Society Recommendation. Her poems have appeared in The New Statesman, T*he Penguin Book of the Prose Poem*, *Poetry Review*, and The Times Literary Supplement. She teaches creative writing at the University of Bristol.

Will Harris lives and works in London. He is the author of the poetry books *RENDANG* (2020) and *Brother Poem* (2023).

Ziddy Ibn Sharam is the deep fake author of *Acharnement* (Distance No Object, 2021) and *Working Museum* (Veer2, 2022).

Robert Kiely is the current Poet-in-Residence at University of Surrey. *simmering of a declarative void* is his first full-length collection, and it was followed by a critical essay, *Incomparable Poetry*, from punctum.

Alice Kinsella was born in Dublin and raised in Co. Mayo, where she now lives. Her poetry pamphlet *Sexy Fruit* (Broken Sleep Books) was a Poetry Book Society Spring 2019 Selection. She edited *Empty House: poetry and prose on the climate crisis* (Doire Press, 2021) Kinsella's creative non-fiction debut *Milk* will be published by Picador in 2023.

Dr Chris Laoutaris is a working-class British-born Greek Cypriot poet, biographer, Shakespeare scholar and Associate Professor at The Shakespeare Institute (University of Birmingham). His first poetry collection, *Bleed and See* (Broken Sleep Books, 2022), was shortlisted for the Eric Gregory Poetry Awards, and his book, *Shakespeare and the Countess: The Battle that Gave Birth to the Globe* (Penguin), was shortlisted for the Tony Lothian Prize, was an *Observer* Book of the Year, *Telegraph* Book of the Year, and a *New York Post* 'Must-Read Book'. His *Shakespeare's Book: The Intertwined Lives Behind the First Folio* is forthcoming from William Collins (2023).

Len Lukowksi is a queer writer and performer based in Glasgow. He writes poetry, fiction, lyrics and memoir. His work has been published in The Quietus, Magma, New Writing Scotland and many other places. In 2018 he won the Wasafiri New Writing Award for Life Writing. Len's debut poetry pamphlet *The Bare Thing* is published by Broken Sleep Books. He has played in the punk bands Jean Genet, Twinken Park and Faggot.

John McCullough lives in Hove. His third book of poems, *Reckless Paper Birds*, was published with Penned in the Margins and won the 2020 Hawthornden Prize for Literature as well as being shortlisted for the Costa Poetry Award. John's previous collections have been Books of the Year for publications including *The Guardian* and *The Independent*, and he also won the Polari First Book Prize. His poem 'Flower of Sulphur' was shortlisted for the 2021 Forward Prize for Best Single Poem. His fourth collection, *Panic Response*, was published in March 2022 by Penned in the Margins.

Andrew McMillan has written three collections of poetry. He lives in Manchester.

Ian McMillan was born in 1956 in the village near Barnsley where he still lives; he's been a freelance writer, performer, and broadcaster since 1981 and has published many collections of poetry for children and adults. He works extensively on radio, presenting The Verb on Radio 3, and, on TV, is a regular on Newsnight Review and Have I Got News for You.

Hollie McNish is a *Sunday Times* bestselling author based between Cambridge and Glasgow. She won the Ted Hughes Award for New Work in Poetry for her poetic parenting memoir – *Nobody Told Me* - of which The Scotsman stated 'The World Needs this Book'. She has published four further collections of poetry – *Papers, Cherry Pie, Plum* and her most recent poetic memoir *Slug...and other things I've been told to hate*, which covers topics from grief to otters, grandmothers to Finnish saunas. She has just completed a re-imagining of Sophocles' Greek Tragedy *Antigone*.She really loves plums and writing poems.

Stuart McPherson is a poet living near Leicester in the UK. Recent poems have appeared in *Butcher's Dog Magazine, Poetry Wales,* and *Anthropocene.* The pamphlet *Waterbearer* was published in December 2021 by Broken Sleep Books. A debut full length collection *Obligate Carnivore* was published by Broken Sleep Books in August 2022.

Jessica Mookherjee is the author of three pamphlets and three full collections of poetry. *Tigress* (Nine Arches Press) was shortlisted for best second collection in the Ledbury Munthe Prize. She has had poems highly commended in the Forward Prize twice (in 2017 & 2021). She is co-editor of Against the Grain Press.

Jeremy Noel-Tod teaches in the School of Literature, Drama and Creative Writing at the University of East Anglia. He has edited *The Oxford Companion to Modern Poetry* (2013), R.F. Langley's *Complete Poems* (2015) and *The Penguin Book of the Prose Poem* (2018). He tweets – no longer about plums – @jntod.

Daniele Pantano is a Swiss poet, essayist, literary translator, and artist. He has published over twenty volumes of poetry, essays, and translations, and his work has been translated into a dozen languages. Pantano is Associate Professor (Reader) and Programme Leader for the MA Creative Writing at the University of Lincoln.

Bobby Parker was born in 1982 in Kidderminster, Worcestershire. His critically acclaimed first full-length poetry collection *Blue Movie* (Nine Arches Press, 2014) was followed by *Working Class Voodoo* (Offord Road Books, 2018), and *Honey Monster* (Broken Sleep Books, 2022). He has taught at The Poetry School and been widely published in magazines in print and online.

Ian Patterson has taught English for almost twenty years at Queens' College, Cambridge. His academic books include *Guernica and Total War* (Profile, 2007). He's published numerous works of poetry, including *Time to Get Here: Selected Poems 1969-2002* (Salt, 2003), *Still Life* (Oystercatcher Press, 2015) and *Bound To Be* (Equipage, 2017).

Michael Pedersen is a prize-winning Scottish poet, scribbler, stitcher. He's unfurled two acclaimed collections of poetry (Polygon Books) with a prose debut, *Boy Friends*, published by Faber & Faber in 2022. He won a Robert Louis Stevenson Fellowship, the John Mather's Trust Rising Star of Literature Award, and was a finalist for the 2018 Writer of the Year at The Herald Scottish Culture Awards. With work anthologised by Pan MacMillan and Canongate Books, Pedersen also co-founded the infamous Neu! Reekie! literary production house.

J. H. Prynne is a British poet closely associated with the British Poetry Revival. Prynne was educated at St Dunstan's College, Catford, and Jesus College, Cambridge. He is a Life Fellow of Gonville and Caius College, Cambridge.

Born and educated in Baddawi refugee camp, **Yousif M. Qasmiyeh** is a poet and translator whose doctoral research at the University of Oxford examines containment and the archive in 'refugee writing'. Time, the body, and ruination inform his poetry and prose, which have appeared in journals including *Modern Poetry in Translation, Stand, Critical Quarterly, GeoHumanities, Cambridge Literary Review,* and Humanities. Yousif is the Creative Encounters Editor of the *Migration and Society* journal, and his collection, *Writing the Camp* (Broken Sleep Books, 2021) was a Poetry Book Society Recommendation, and was shortlisted for the Royal Society of Literature's Ondaatje Prize.

Gita Ralleigh is a writer, poet and doctor born to Indian immigrant parents in London. Her poetry has been published by *Magma Poetry, The Rialto, Poetry Birmingham* and *The North* among others. Her debut pamphlet *A Terrible Thing* was published by Bad Betty Press in 2020 and her second pamphlet, *Siren*, by Broken Sleep Books in August 2022. She is a member of the Kinara poetry collective and a trustee at Spread The Word.

Sam Riviere won an Eric Gregory Award in 2009, and the Forward Prize for Best First Collection in 2012 for 81 Austerities. Since 2015 he has run the independent press If a Leaf Falls Press in Edinburgh, and in 2021, Riviere's first novel, *Dead Souls* was published by Weidenfeld & Nicolson.

Peter Scalpello is a queer poet and therapist from Glasgow. Their work has appeared in *Five Dials, Granta*, and *The London Magazine*, among other publications. Their pamphlets *Acting Out / chem & other poems* are published by Broken Sleep Books. Peter's debut collection, *Limbic*, is published by Cipher Press. Twitter @p_scalpello.

Penelope Shuttle's work is widely anthologised and can be heard on The Poetry Archive Website. Her poetry has been broadcast on BBC Radio 3 and 4, and her poem 'Outgrown' was used recently in a radio and television commercial. She has been a judge for many poetry competitions, is a Hawthornden Fellow, and a tutor for the Poetry School. She is current Chair of the Falmouth Poetry Group, one of the longest-running poetry workshops in the country.

Maria Sledmere is a poet, artist and critic based in Glasgow, where she also teaches. She is editor-in-chief of SPAM Press and a member of the art and ecology collective, A+E. Her debut collection, *The Luna Erratum*, is out now with Dostoyevsky Wannabe. Recent publications include *Sans Soleil*, a collaboration with fred spoliar (Face Press/Mermaid Motel, 2022), and *String Feeling* (Erotoplasty Editions, 2022). She is co-editor of *the weird folds: everyday poems from the anthropocene* (Dostoyevsky Wannabe, 2020). Find her at mariasledmere.com.

Taran Spalding-Jenkin is an award-winning poet who has performed from Cornwall to Connemara, using Kernewek and English to explore health, identity, and folklore. Since 2019 he has co-organised and hosted Bristol Tonic and has facilitated bilingual creative workshops with schools and community groups across the South West. He has been published in *Poetry Wales, The Poets' Republic, 26 Voices for Change, Cornish Modern Poetries*, and produced *A Shanty For Cornish Youth* for BBC Arts, which won a Gorsedh Kernow award in 2021. His debut poetry pamphlet will be published by Broken Sleep Books in 2023.

Ross Sutherland was born in Edinburgh in 1979. He is the author of four collections of poetry, including *Things To Do Before You Leave Town* and *Emergency Window*. His theatre credits include *Stand By For Tape Back-Up* (2015) and the palindromic play *Party Trap* (2018). He also produces the experimental audio-fiction podcast, Imaginary Advice.

Rob Taylor is the author of four poetry collections and the editor of the anthologies *What the Poets Are Doing: Canadian Poets in Conversation* and *Best Canadian Poetry 2019*, but everyone just knows him as that annoying plum guy on Twitter. The arc of his literary life was completed upon his publication in this anthology.

U. G. Világos is a poet, editor and teacher, well known for his collection *The Lark Sings Wind*. His new collection, *The Mostly Fictitious Man*, is forthcoming in Summer 2023, and a collection of flash-poems titled *Troubles, Nights, Meditations & Memoranda for a Passing Smile* is forthcoming in 2024. He is the editor of *We Still Use Poetry: The 2nd Quarterly Anthology of Contemporary Poetry in the Margins*.

Ed Wall is a musician, editor and English teacher from London.

John Welson has participated in over 300 exhibitions in both private and public galleries around the world. From the late 1960's to the early 1990's he painted Figurative Surrealist Paintings, exhibiting with artists as diverse as Salvador Dali, Man Ray, Rene Magritte, Max Ernst, Lucian Freud and Damian Hirst. Since the mid 1990's he has produced Lyrical Abstracted Paintings inspired by the landscape of his native Wales.

Chrissy Williams is based in south-east London and her second collection *LOW* was published by Bloodaxe in 2021.

This is just to say I have laid out my unrest